The Digestive System

by Helen Frost

Consulting Editor: Gail Saunders-Smith, Ph.D.

Consultant: Lawrence M. Ross, M.D., Ph.D.
Member, American Association of Clinical Anatomists

Pebble Books

an imprint of Capstone Press
Mankato, Minnesota

Pebble Books are published by Capstone Press
151 Good Counsel Drive, P.O. Box 669, Mankato, Minnesota 56002
http://www.capstone-press.com

1 2 3 4 5 6 06 05 04 03 02 01

Library of Congress Cataloging-in-Publication Data
Frost, Helen, 1949–
    The digestive system/by Helen Frost.
    p. cm.—(Human body systems)
    Includes bibliographical references and index.
    Summary: Introduces the various parts of the digestive system and the
functions they perform.
    ISBN 0-7368-0649-0
    1. Digestive organs—Juvenile literature. [1. Digestive system.] I. Title. II. Human
body systems (Mankato, Minn.)
QM301 .F76 2001
611′.3—dc21

                                                                    00-026997

Note to Parents and Teachers

The Human Body Systems series supports national science standards for units on understanding the basic functions of the human body. This book describes the digestive system and illustrates its purpose, parts, and functions. The photographs and diagrams support early readers in understanding the text. This book also introduces early readers to subject-specific vocabulary words, which are defined in the Words to Know section. Early readers may need assistance to read some words and to use the Table of Contents, Words to Know, Read More, Internet Sites, and Index/Word List sections of the book.

Table of Contents

4

The digestive system changes food so the body can use it. Digestion breaks food into tiny parts.

Digestion begins in the mouth. Teeth bite and chew food. Saliva makes food soft.

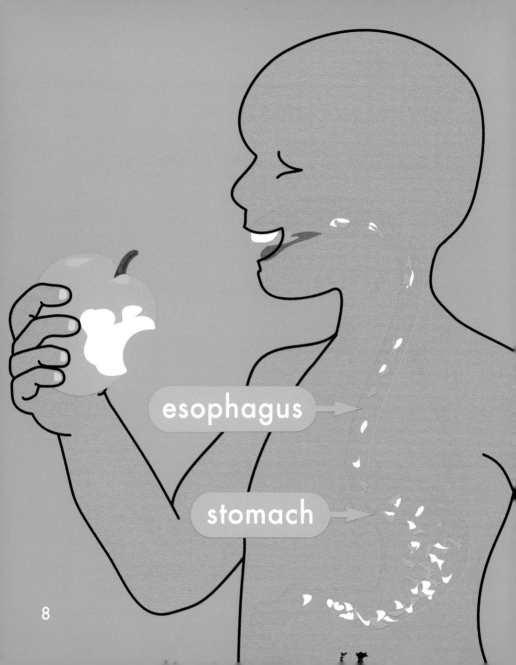

esophagus →

stomach →

8

Swallowed food goes into the esophagus. The esophagus is a tube between the mouth and the stomach.

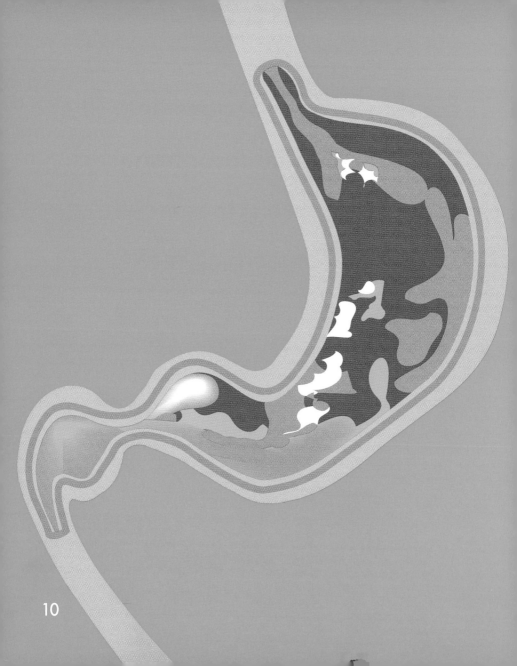

Food moves through the
esophagus into the stomach.
The stomach mixes the
food. The food becomes
a thick paste.

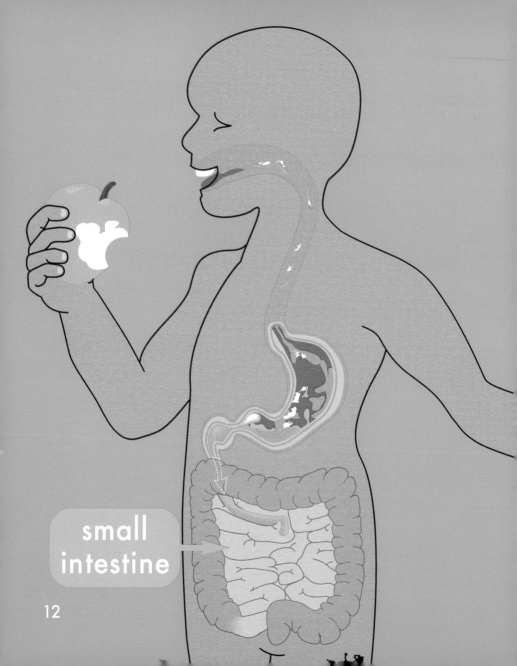

small
intestine

The stomach moves the food
into the small intestine.
The small intestine is a
long winding tube.

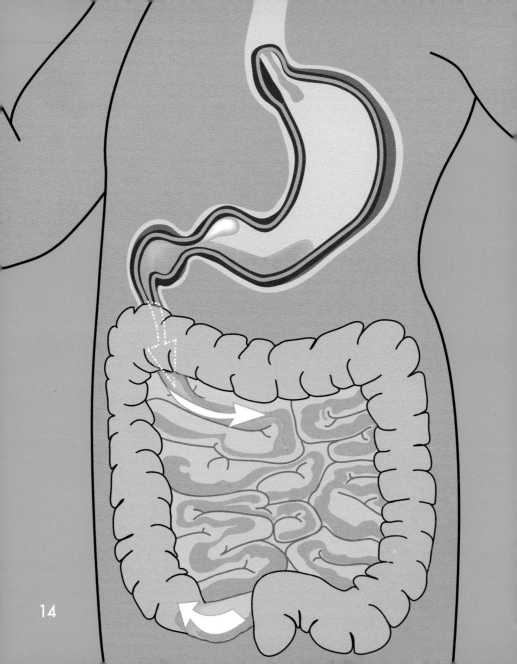

Food slowly moves through the small intestine. Enzymes help break the food into tiny parts. The food becomes a liquid.

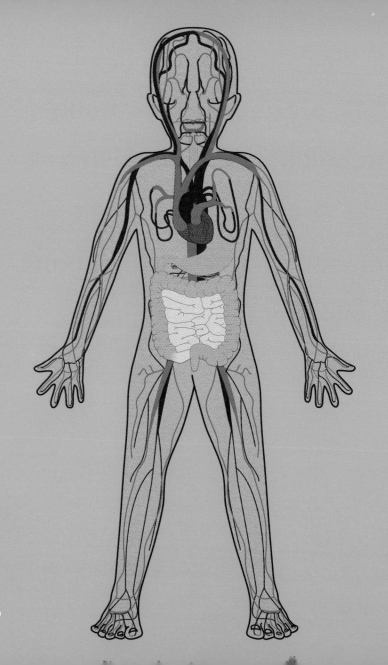

The body absorbs the parts of the food it needs. The food parts go into the blood. Blood carries the food parts to all areas of the body.

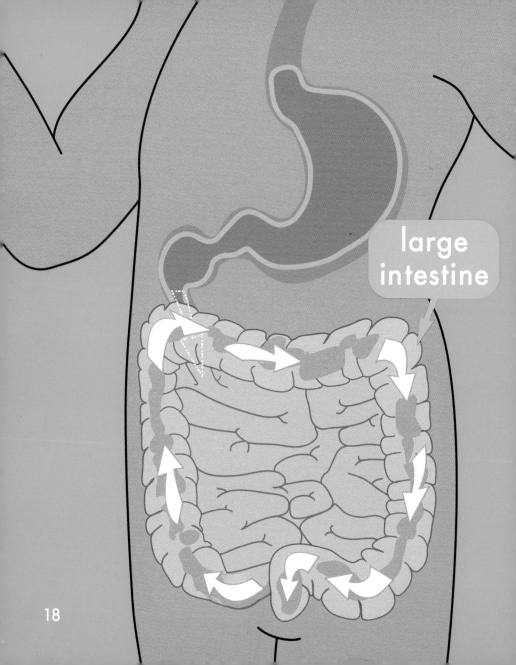

large
intestine

18

The body does not use some parts of the food. This waste matter moves into the large intestine. The large intestine pushes the waste matter out of the body.

Food gives the body energy. It helps people think, move, and grow.

Words to Know

enzyme—a substance that helps break down food

esophagus—the tube that carries food from the mouth to the stomach; muscles in the esophagus push food into the stomach.

large intestine—a tube that is the last part of the digestive system; the large intestine pushes solid waste matter out of the body.

saliva—the clear liquid in the mouth; an enzyme in saliva begins to break down food.

small intestine—a long tube between the stomach and the large intestine; the small intestine is coiled to fit in the body; digested food in the small intestine passes into the bloodstream.

stomach—the place where chewed food is broken down; the stomach uses gastric juices to digest food; gastric juices are made of water, acid, and enzymes.

Read More

Ballard, Carol. *The Stomach and Digestive System.*
The Human Body. Austin, Texas: Raintree
Steck-Vaughn, 1997.

Parker, Steve. *Digestion.* Look at Your Body.
Brookfield, Conn.: Copper Beech Books, 1997.

Stille, Darlene R. *The Digestive System.* A True Book.
New York: Children's Press, 1997.

Internet Sites

The Food Factory: The Digestive System
http://www.imcpl.lib.in.us/nov_dig.htm

The Real Deal on the Digestive System
http://kidshealth.org/kid/body/digest_noSW.html

Your Gross and Cool Body—Digestive System
http://www.yucky.com/body/index.ssf?/
systems/digestion/

Index/Word List

Word Count: 173
Early-Intervention Level: 18

Editorial Credits

Martha E. H. Rustad, editor; Kia Bielke, designer; Marilyn Moseley LaMantia, Graphicstock, illustrator; Katy Kudela, photo researcher

Photo Credits

Index Stock Imagery/Myrleen Ferguson Cate, 20
International Stock/Mitch Diamond, 4
Kathy Ferguson/Pictor, 6
Photo Network/Eric R. Berndt, 1
Shaffer Photography/James L. Shaffer, cover

The author thanks the children's section staff at the Allen County Public Library in Fort Wayne, Indiana, for research assistance. The author also thanks Linda Hathaway, CFCS, Health Educator, McMillen Center for Health Education, Fort Wayne, Indiana.